FOOTBALL LEGENDS

Troy Aikman

Terry Bradshaw

Jim Brown

Dan Marino

Joe Montana

Joe Namath

Walter Payton

Jerry Rice

Barry Sanders

Deion Sanders

Emmitt Smith

Steve Young

CHELSEA HOUSE PUBLISHERS

FOOTBALL LEGENDS

TROY AIKMAN

Richard Rosenblatt

Introduction by
Chuck Noll

CHELSEA HOUSE PUBLISHERS
New York · Philadelphia

Produced by Daniel Bial and Associates
New York, New York

Picture research by Alan Gottlieb
Cover illustration by Bill Vann

3 5 7 9 8 6 4 2

Rosenblatt, Richard.
     Troy Aikman / by Richard Rosenblatt.
     p. cm.—(Football legends)
     Includes bibliographical references and index.
     Summary: A biography of the star quarterback, from his
     childhood in California through his college days at the
     University of Oklahoma to his professional career with the
     Dallas Cowboys.
     ISBN 0-7910-2457-1
     1. Aikman, Troy, 1966—Juvenile literature. 2. Football
     players—United States—Biography—Juvenile literature. 3.
     Dallas Cowboys (Football team)—Juvenile literature. [1.
     Aikman, Troy,
     1966- . 2. Football players.] I. Title II. Series.
     GV939.a46R67 1996
     796.332'092—dc20
     [B]   95-18223
                                                         CIP
                                                          AC

CONTENTS

A WINNING ATTITUDE

Chuck Noll

Don't ever fall into the trap of believing, "I could never do that. And I won't even try—I don't want to embarrass myself." After all, most top athletes had no idea what they could accomplish when they were young. A secret to the success of every star quarterback and sure-handed receiver is that they tried. If they had not tried, if they had not persevered, they would never have discovered how far they could go and how much they could achieve.

You can learn about trying hard and overcoming challenges by being a sports fan. Or you can take part in organized sports at any level, in any capacity. The student messenger at my high school is now president of a university. A reserve ballplayer who got very little playing time in high school now owns a very successful business. Both of them benefited by the lesson of perseverance that sports offers. The main point is that you don't have to be a Hall of Fame athlete to reap the benefits of participating in sports.

In math class, I learned that the whole is equal to the sum of its parts. But that is not always the case when you are dealing with people. Sports has taught me that the whole is either greater than or less than the sum of its parts, depending on how well the parts work together. And how the parts work together depends on how they really understand the concept of teamwork.

Most people believe that teamwork is a fifty-fifty proposition. But true teamwork is seldom, if ever, fifty-fifty. Teamwork is *whatever it takes to get the job done*. There is no time for the measurement of contributions, no time for anything but concentrating on your job.

One year, my Pittsburgh Steelers were playing the Houston Oilers in the Astrodome late in the season, with the division championship on the line. Our offensive line was hard hit by the flu, our starting quarterback was out with an injury, and we were having difficulty making a first down. There was tremendous pressure on our defense to perform well—and they rose to the occasion. If the players on the defensive unit had been measuring their contribution against the offense's contribution, they would have given up and gone home. Instead, with a "whatever it takes" attitude, they increased their level of concentration and performance, forced turnovers, and got the ball into field goal range for our offense. Thanks to our defense's winning attitude, we came away with a victory.

Believing in doing whatever it takes to get the job done is what separates a successful person from someone who is not as successful. Nobody can give you this winning outlook; you have to develop it. And I know from experience that it can be learned and developed on the playing field.

My favorite people on the football field have always been offensive linemen and defensive backs. I say this because it takes special people to perform well in jobs in which there is little public recognition when they are doing things right but are thrust into the spotlight as soon as they make a mistake. That is exactly what happens to a lineman whose man sacks the quarterback or a defensive back who lets his receiver catch a touchdown pass. They know the importance of being part of a group that believes in teamwork and does not point fingers at one another.

Sports can be a learning situation as much as it can be fun. And that's why I say, "Get involved. Participate."

CHUCK NOLL, the Pittsburgh Steelers head coach from 1969–1991, led his team to four Super Bowl victories—the most by any coach. Widely respected as an innovator on both offense and defense, Noll was inducted into the Pro Football Hall of Fame in 1993.

1

AIKMAN'S GREATEST GAME

It almost seemed as if Troy Aikman was waiting for a Super Bowl stage to shed all the "can't-win-the-big-game tags" he was slapped with over the years, be it a subpar performance in the Rose Bowl or a loss to bitter rival Southern Cal with the Rose Bowl on the line. Sure, he suffered the aches and pains of a rebuilding franchise when he joined the Dallas Cowboys, and helped get them into the playoffs in just his third season under the superb tutelage of coach Jimmy Johnson.

But nothing could prepare his critics, not to mention his backers, for his performance of a lifetime in the 1993 Super Bowl, played at the Rose Bowl in Pasadena, California. It was Troy's greatest game, and even though his Cowboys won the Super Bowl again the following season, it was his exploits in his first Super Bowl that put him in a class with the best in NFL history.

Dallas Cowboy's quarterback Troy Aikman drops back to pass in Super Bowl XXVII.

Simply put, Aikman was marvelous. His classic drop back style, his confident release, and his emotional leadership led to one of the best clutch performances in sports. The Buffalo Bills, who were trying for a third straight year to win the Super Bowl, had to be awed by Aikman's uncanny ability to hit one of his many talented receivers whenever he needed to. (The Cowboys beat the Bills in the 1994 Super Bowl, too.)

The score, 52–17, led the "Tonight Show" host Jay Leno to remark to Aikman on his show the night after: "Fifty-two to 17? Fifty-two to 17? I mean, is that a football score?"

Aikman was awesome, completing 22 of 30 passes for 273 yards and 4 touchdowns. He was the Super Bowl's Most Valuable Player and the folks at Disney had him scream (for $60,000) into a camera: "I'm going to Disneyland," followed by "I'm going to Disney World," for an advertisement that began running the following day.

On January 31, 1993, Aikman and the Cowboys arrived at the Rose Bowl unaware that Johnson had told his coaches Dallas couldn't lose. After all, Aikman had thrown 59 passes, 4 going for touchdowns, without an interception in playoff victories over the Philadelphia Eagles and the San Francisco 49ers in the NFC championship game. And Johnson, always the strategist, truly believed with stars like Aikman, Emmitt Smith, and Michael Irvin, his team was invincible. Boy, was he right.

It rained the Saturday night before the Super Bowl, clearing the smog out of the area and making for a brilliant Sunday at the Rose Bowl. A cleaner, clearer, crisper day couldn't have been had.

"It was a gorgeous day," Aikman recalled in *The Boys,* a book about the Cowboys' 1992–93 season. "I was still feeling very relaxed. I think most guys were relaxed but very focused."

Until they trotted onto the field for warmups.

A hit by Bills linebacker Darryl Talley prompts Aikman to take another look at the game. But the Cowboys had the last laugh in Super Bowl XVII.

Tight end Lin Elliott fell twice. Aikman had so much trouble setting himself to throw, he had to change to longer cleats.

"But other than that I was great," Aikman said. "I was amazed because I kept waiting for the nerves to kick in. I felt like I was warming up before any other game. It just wouldn't hit me that this was the Super Bowl."

That feeling lasted only until it got closer to game time. The Rose Bowl was jammed with 98,374 people, many of whom paid the going rate of $175 per ticket, but many, many others paying as high as $1,000 a ticket for a chance to watch a game worthy of two weeks of hype.

When Aikman was introduced to the crowd, he recalled: "All of a sudden I let myself get caught up in the excitement. I was actually hyperventilating."

When Garth Brooks sang the National Anthem and the five jet fighters flew over the stadium, the crowd roared and the Cowboys were awed.

After forcing the Bills to punt on the opening series, Aikman lined up behind the center with a third and 9 at his own 16 yardline. He dropped back and his pass landed 40 yards upfield. The intended receiver, Michael Irvin, was only 10 yards away. Said offensive coordinator Norv Turner: "Troy looked pretty jittery."

It got worse. Mike Saxon's punt was blocked by Steve Tasker, the Bills recovered on the Cowboys' 16, Thurman Thomas scored on a 2-yard run and Buffalo quickly led 7–0.

The Bills looked to be driving again, but Jim Kelly threw a fluttery pass that was intercepted by James Washington and Aikman and Co. were back in business. With a third and 16 at his own 47, Aikman threw a bullet to Irvin for 20 yards and a first down. It was the pass that turned around Aikman's game.

"That pass really loosened Troy up," Turner said.

Two plays later, on a play called "scat right 370 F shoot pump," Aikman threw a perfect spiral to tight end Jay Novacek for a 23-yard touchdown pass. It was 7–7 and Aikman was finally at ease.

The Bills took over, but not for long, as defensive end Jimmie Jones caught a Jim Kelly fumble at the Buffalo 2 yardline and scored to make it 14–7 Cowboys.

Three series later Kelly suffered a sprained knee and missed the rest of the game. Frank Reich took over and he guided the Bills to a field goal to cut the lead to 14–10.

But Aikman had his confidence back and he had a feeling the Cowboys were ready to open up the game.

"I was really getting comfortable with the flow of the game," he said. "Some games start out 100 miles per hour, then slow way down. But then it was like [their defensive] players were playing half speed. Buffalo had cut it to 4 but I was feeling like we were up 30 because I just didn't think they could stop our offense."

The Cowboys took over and Aikman capped a drive mixed with Smith runs and several key completions with a 19-yard touchdown pass to Irvin. Twenty-one to 10, Cowboys.

Tony Wise, the Cowboys offensive line coach who is now an assistant with the Chicago Bears, recalled thinking: "I would hate to have to play the Dallas Cowboys. Troy Aikman is playing with a confidence very few players feel."

The Most Valuable Player in the 1993 Super Bowl exults after proving he could win the big one after all.

Now the Cowboys were rolling. Thomas fumbled after a hit by Leon Lett, and the Cowboys went for it all. Aikman, throwing off-balance and quicker than he wanted to, hit Irvin for an 18-yard touchdown and it was 28–10. As quick as that. At halftime, the Cowboys were up 18 points.

Aikman was so excited, he uncharacteristically ran down toward the end zone holding his index finger in the air. Even Coach Johnson was psyched, running into the lockerroom pumping both fists into the air.

It was only halftime, and Aikman had taken over the game.

The second half was more of the same, and you had to be a Cowboys fan to stick with the game the rest of the way. Or, as many people did, you stayed with the game to see how Aikman would finish up.

The Bills made it 31–17 at one point, but Aikman took care of that, tossing his longest touchdown pass of the day—a 45-yarder to Alvin Harper—to push the score to 38–17. After that, Smith scored from 10 yards out and, two plays later, linebacker Ken Norton, Jr., scooped up a fumble and ran 9 yards for another touchdown.

"The only thing that could stop the Cowboys is an earthquake in Santa Monica," said Buffalo's wide receiver James Lofton.

It must be noted that the score was almost 59–17. Near the end of the game, Leon Lett, the Cowboys' 300-pound defensive lineman, picked up a fumble and started to rumble down the sidelines for a sure touchdown. After running 64 yards, and just as he was about to cross the goal line, he slowed down and raised his arms in triumph—and was stripped of the ball by the never-say-die Don Beebe. Whether he was trying to enjoy the moment or had run out of gas, Lett was completely surprised by the Bills' small wide receiver, the only man who had even bothered to try to run after Lett.

While Smith finished with 22 carries for 108 yards and six catches for 27 more yards, and Irvin had six catches for 114 yards and 2 touchdowns, Aikman was the MVP. In three playoff games, Aikman was an amazing 61 of 89 for 795 yards and 8 touchdowns. His playoff rating of 116.7 broke the all time mark of the legendary Green Bay quarterback, Bart Starr.

Not bad for a guy who can't win the big one.

"This game means everything to me," Aikman said. "A tremendous weight has been lifted off my shoulders. No matter what happens the rest of my career, I can say I took a team to a Super Bowl and won it. There aren't too many who can say that.

"This is as great a feeling as I've ever had in my life."

Aikmania had swept through Texas. It was about to sweep the nation.

2

THE EARLY YEARS

He was born Troy Kenneth Aikman on November 21, 1966, and grew up in Cerritos, California, the youngest of Ken and Charlyn's three children. The first Super Bowl was played two months later.

Right from birth, Aikman had to struggle. When his parents noticed Troy's legs were slightly bowed below the knees and his toes curled under his feet, they took him to the doctor. Dr. Bill McColl, a former Chicago Bears player, diagnosed Troy as having a mild form of clubfoot.

McColl had Aikman's feet put in casts when he was eight months old. They were changed every two weeks. He wore them until he began walking at 14 months, actually learning how to walk with the casts.

He also had to wear specially designed shoes—the toes pointed out like they were on the wrong feet—until he was three years old. His

Aikman was already a standout football player as a junior at Henryetta High School.

feet were strapped together when he slept.

His feet began to grow normally and Aikman eventually began to play sports, especially baseball and touch football. He also played basketball with his older sisters, Terri and Tammy.

While Aikman was growing up, his father worked long hours in the pipeline construction business. And in 1979, when Aikman was 12, the family moved from California to Henryetta, Oklahoma, (population 6,000) where they lived on a 172-acre ranch with cows, pigs, and chickens.

This was quite a change for Aikman, who was about to enter the eighth grade. No more trips to the mall on the bike. There wasn't one in Henryetta.

"We had no neighbors," Aikman said. "I didn't like Oklahoma at all."

Of course, he changed his tune once school began and he met kids his own age.

But even before the move to Oklahoma, some of Aikman's coaches recalled his younger days.

Manny Jesolva, a coach in the Pee Wee football league in the Cerritos area, probably was the first person to make Aikman a No. 1 draft pick. Aikman was 10.

"I saw him as a 9-year-old and he did very well," said Jesolva, who was general manager of a vending company at the time. "I think they took the junior pee-wee championship that year. I had the first pick in the draft the next year, so I got to get him.

"It wasn't really hard to tell he would succeed. He threw the ball well. He didn't know how to release very well."

But Rod Davis, the assistant coach, worked

with Aikman.

"One of the things we tried to teach him is to carry out his fakes," he said. "He's probably one of the best in the country at that. He could throw the ball accurately 30 yards as a nine-year-old. He was always taller, and he played up a level. He was larger than average. Troy was a perfect passer for as long as I can remember."

The pair also recalled several injuries to Aikman. Davis said when Aikman was 10 or 11, he broke his wrist at practice.

"We put an airbag on it and took him to the hospital. There was not a whimper, no concern about the injury. In fact, he was playing as a linebacker, so he was tough," he said.

Jesolva thought Aikman broke his growth bone, which could have ended his hopes of becoming a professional athlete. Luckily, that wasn't the case.

A year later, the Aikmans moved to Oklahoma.

After a season of junior high football, Aikman started at Henryetta High School, a Class 3A school in the small town south of Tulsa.

Besides football, the young Aikman also excelled at basketball and baseball.

Bill Holt coached the Fighting Hens for four seasons, and Rick Enis coached the receivers. In Aikman's junior year, the team went 2-8, winning the last two games and making the playoffs. His senior year, the Fighting Hens were 6-4 but did not make the playoffs.

"It was the school's first playoff team in 25 years," Aikman said. "'Two and eight and going to the state' was our slogan. Although we lost in the first round, we changed tradition."

Ninth-graders didn't play on the varsity, but already Aikman was ahead of most of the quarterbacks when he got to high school.

"When we would work on fundamental skills, all of the things we were trying to teach the older kids, Troy already did," Holt said.

"Troy didn't have a whole lot of touch (then), but the ball was always on the mark. The receivers were all smaller. I saw a lot of them get hit in the face mask."

Aikman was 17 when he was a senior, a bit younger then most of the football players.

"He never looked like a little kid," recalled Holt. "When most of the 13- and 14-year-olds were playing backyard football behind the stands, he was starting for a 3A team. Troy always seemed to have a lot of maturity.

"Against Hartshorne High, we were seven points down in the last two minutes of the game. We were throwing the ball. Two of Hartshorne's guys had him and were taking him down. As Troy was falling, from a sidearm position, he threw a 25-yard touchdown pass. I live near Hartshorne now. The kids still talk about it.

"We still lost by a point, but after the game, their coach told Troy: 'We'll be watching you someday on Monday Night Football.'"

Aikman also became a Dallas Cowboys fan and admirer of quarterback Roger Staubach. The Aikman ranch was about 200 miles north of Dallas.

And, although he lived there only five years before leaving to go to college at Oklahoma University, Aikman still calls Henryetta home, the place where he acquired a down-to-earth charm.

"I've never tried to be anything that I'm not," he says. "I understand my place in the world and where football fits. Everybody searches for inner peace. Some are able to have it, some aren't.

"People criticize me for not being emotional, for not smiling enough. If someone sees me smiling, I'm happy. If not, I don't feel like it. Like smiling for pictures with fans. I can't turn it on and off like that. I'm very content with who I am and what I am. I'm not trying to be something people want me to be."

Before he went to college though, Aikman, who also played baseball in high school, briefly considered a pro career as a shortstop or pitcher. Before the baseball draft of 1984, he heard that the New York Mets were interested in him. A scout called and asked how much money it would take to sign him.

A few years before, Aikman would have played for free. But since he already had decided to play football at Oklahoma, he told the scout "I'd probably sign for $200,000."

The scout wasn't interested and it was on to Boomer Sooner land to play for coach Barry Switzer.

3

COLLEGE CREDITS

By his senior season at Henryetta High School, Troy was an all-state quarterback and one of the nation's most highly sought players. In a fantastic senior season, Troy threw for 3,208 yards and ran for another 1,568 yards. Everyone wanted Troy, but living in Oklahoma for five years had given Sooners coach Barry Switzer an advantage. Even over Oklahoma State coach Jimmy Johnson.

"I'd been in Oklahoma since I was 12," Aikman explained. "In the state of Oklahoma, OU football is everything. Everybody wants to go to OU. When I was coming out of high school, Oklahoma was running the I [formation], and coach Switzer told me that they were going to stay in the I. And I believed him."

So Aikman signed a letter of intent to go to school in Norman, with dreams of winning even more national championships for the beloved

Coach Barry Switzer suggested to Aikman he'd be a star at Oklahoma. It didn't happen that way, though.

Oklahoma Sooners. And he would be the player to guide them.

It never happened. As soon as Aikman made Oklahoma his choice, Switzer changed his game plan. With star running back Marcus Dupree gone, Switzer gave up on the I and said the Sooners were going back to the wishbone.

As a freshman, Aikman played briefly when the two quarterbacks ahead of him were hurt. As a sophomore, he led the Sooners to three victories before University of Miami defensive tackle Jerome Brown sacked Aikman and broke his leg in the fourth game of the season.

At that point, Switzer inserted Jamelle Holieway into the lineup. Holieway was the perfect wishbone quarterback, and he proved it by leading the Sooners to a terrific season. Switzer saw no reason to go back to Aikman and the quarterback knew what he had to do.

"When I went to coach Switzer to tell him that I wanted to transfer, he told me he'd been expecting me," Aikman recalled. "He told me he thought it would be best for me, but that he didn't think it was his place to say it, like he was asking me to leave. But he didn't think I'd have to waste the rest of my college career. So he made some calls for me."

One of them went to UCLA coach Terry Donahue. Like he told others, Switzer informed Donahue that Aikman would be a good pro quarterback someday but he just didn't fit into the Oklahoma wishbone. When Donahue heard that a 6'3", 217-pound quarterback with a strong arm and a knack for reading defenses was available, he had a hard time concealing his joy.

The Aikman-UCLA fit was a natural one.

Aikman may still call Oklahoma home, but he was born in West Covina, a suburb of Los Angeles. In addition, Troy's father had just taken a job in Riverside, California, (an hour's drive from Los Angeles) because business was slow in Oklahoma. His mother, though, remained in Henryetta, where she was a type-setter for the *Henryetta Daily Free-Lance.*

During his redshirt season, Aikman studied the complex Bruins' offense with volunteer coach Rick Neuheisel, who played for UCLA and led the team to a 1984 Rose Bowl win over Illinois. Neuheisel, now the coach at the University of Colorado, remembers,"Troy has everything I didn't have—size, speed, and a great arm."

Aikman learned well. In his first season at UCLA, he established himself as one of the nation's best quarterbacks. First, he beat out the popular Brendan McCracken, who had been at UCLA for three years, for the starting job. Through 10 games, Aikman led the nation in passing efficiency, and had only three intercep-tions (two were deflected) as the Bruins lost only to the University of Nebraska.

Aikman had the Bruins in position to play in the Rose Bowl before having his worst game of the season against archrival USC. Against the Trojans, he threw three interceptions, USC won 17–13, tied the Bruins for the Pacific-10 Conference and earned the Rose Bowl berth.

But Aikman ended his first season at UCLA on a high note, passing for 173 yards and a touchdown in a victory over the University of Florida in the Aloha Bowl.

For the season, Aikman had amassed some amazing numbers: 159 of 243 (65.4 percent) for

Aikman's biggest game in college was also his worst. USC picked off three passes on the way to beating UCLA 31–22—and depriving the Bruins of a trip to the Rose Bowl in 1988.

2,354 yards and 16 touchdowns. He was a second-team All-American and the Pac 10's All-Conference quarterback.

Aikman's demeanor remained consistent. He was patient and calm in victory as well as in defeat. After the USC loss, he answered question after question, but never showed how much the loss really hurt. Until later.

"That USC game never has left my mind," Aikman said as he prepared for his second and final season at UCLA. "For two weeks straight after that game, I didn't get any sleep. That was one of the worst losses I've ever suffered as a player."

The start of the 1988 season had less pressure in one sense, and more in another.

Aikman was UCLA's first returning starter at quarterback since 1982, and for the first time, he was not trying to outplay someone to win a starting job. However, he was one of the Heisman Trophy favorites, along with USC quarterback Rodney Peete, who outdueled him the previous season. Also, UCLA had 13 of its players drafted by the NFL.

Nonetheless, Coach Donahue sensed this could be a special season.

"His greatest asset is he has an incredibly strong arm," said Donahue. "He puts tremendous heat on the ball. He can throw off-balance and he has tremendous ball speed. He can put it through cracks between defenders. He also has toughness and competitiveness and good leadership qualities. He has everything a great player has to have. The only thing he doesn't have is a tremendous wealth of experience."

UCLA started off as if it were ready to win a national championship, rolling to seven straight victories to open the season, including a sensational 41–28 win over Nebraska.

After a 34–30 loss to Washington State University, though, the Bruins lost their edge but still managed to eke out victories over

Oregon and Stanford universities.

Aikman, too, was in a funk, throwing for just 249 yards in those wins. But he still had thrown for 2,282 yards and 21 touchdowns in leading the Bruins to a 9-1 record and No. 6 ranking in the Associated Press poll.

And just like last season, it came down to a final showdown against Southern Cal. UCLA was ranked No. 6 coming into the game and USC was ranked No. 2. The winner would get to play the University of Michigan on New Year's Day.

Before the game, Aikman talked about his season.

"I'm not in this for any individual honors," he said. "It would be nice to win the Heisman Trophy and all that, but it's not something I've thought about a lot. If we go out there and win this ballgame, if I don't win the Heisman, that's fine. I want to go to the Rose Bowl. We've played all season to get ourselves in this position."

But once again, UCLA fell short despite a record-setting performance by Aikman, who set a school mark with 32 completions in 48 attempts for 317 yards and 2 touchdowns. Led again by Peete, who had the measles in the week leading up to the game, USC prevailed 31–22.

While Aikman was clearly upset about the loss, his coach and Southern Cal coach Larry Smith knew who the best player was that day.

"It was a superhuman effort," Smith said of Aikman. "If that wasn't a Heisman Trophy effort, I don't know what is."

Added Donahue: "I was very proud of Troy's performance. He played his heart out and it was a very strong performance. He had a brilliant

season and had a great game today, but it's a pity we couldn't win the game for him."

Aikman finished third behind Barry Sanders and Peete in the Heisman Trophy balloting, but

In Aikman's last collegiate game, on January 3, 1989, he helped his team beat the University of Arkansas in the Cotton Bowl, 17–3.

he was a consensus All-American and also won the Davey O'Brien Award as the nation's best quarterback. He finished the season with 2,599 yards and 23 touchdowns while completing 64 percent of his passes.

The quarterback still had one more game to play—against the University of Arkansas in the Cotton Bowl. It seemed only fitting that Aikman would end his college career in a National Football League city already being consumed with Aikmania. That city was Dallas, where the Cowboys had completed a disastrous 3-13 season, but owned the first pick in the league's college player draft.

Cotton Bowl week was like no other for Aikman. He was the talk of the town, and interviewers couldn't get enough of the good-looking kid from tiny Henryetta, Oklahoma, who starred at glamorous UCLA. Even the Arkansas players were envious. "Every time you turn on the TV, you see Aikman doing all the interviews," Arkansas quarterback Quinn Grovey said.

For Aikman, his dream of playing in the NFL was right in front of him. His team practiced at Texas Stadium, home of the Cowboys, and even the Cowboys coach Tom Landry himself showed up to watch Aikman work out.

"It hit me driving into the stadium, when I saw all the names of the legends on the wall, that I might play here someday. I'd love to play for the Cowboys. Of course, all the history would mean a lot more to me if they draft me."

First things first. He wanted to end his career with a victory. He got it with a 17–3 win over Arkansas in the Cotton Bowl—the seventh consecutive bowl win for the Bruins. But the pressure finally seemed to get to Aikman, who came out tight. His final numbers weren't bad, as he completed 19 of 27 passes for 172 yards and a touchdown. But it was the Bruins' running game that took control.

"Troy was tight for the game, and understandably so," Donahue said. "We wanted to take some pressure off him by running the ball some."

Said Gil Brandt, who was the Cowboys personnel director at the time: "Coach Landry will be the one who makes the final decision, but I would be shocked if we don't pick Troy Aikman."

4

THE COWBOYS: THE BUILDING YEARS

After his college exploits, it was time for Aikman to reap the rewards for all his hard work. It was January 1989, and Aikman was the hottest commodity in the upcoming National Football League draft.

In fact, he was in a position to become the NFL's highest paid rookie and call signals for the team he idolized, the team that in the 1960s had become known as "America's Team."

Because the Cowboys finished the 1988 season with a record of 3-13—the league's worst—they were awarded the first pick in the draft. With so much at stake, Aikman hired one of the best agents in the business. Leigh Steinberg was known as the agent of the quarterbacks and Aikman was about to be the quarterback of the

Pete Rozelle (right) began the annual college draft by posing with the No. 1 pick, Troy Aikman. Aikman had already signed a six year, $11.2 million contract with the Dallas Cowboys.

Tom Landry, then the only coach the Cowboys had ever had in their history, had led Dallas to three Super Bowls by 1989.

future for one lucky team.

"The classic paradox in pro football is the most promising prospect often ends up with the team with the most problems," Steinberg said.

He was right. In many ways.

The Dallas Cowboys weren't just any team, especially in 1989. When Arkansas oilman Jerry Jones purchased the team for $140 million in February, he shocked the sports world by firing the legendary Tom Landry, the only coach the Cowboys had ever had. He hired his college chum Jimmy Johnson, who had previously lost out twice in recruiting battles to sign Aikman, first at Oklahoma State and later at the University of Miami.

So now it was the Jerry and Jimmy Show and the football world was watching.

Of course, both immediately fell in love with Aikman, who had grown to 6' 2½" and weighed 218 pounds, and was the quarterback of their dreams.

So it came as no surprise on April 19, four days before the draft, when the Cowboys made it official: Troy Aikman was their man.

"I'm really looking forward to becoming a Dallas Cowboy," were Aikman's first words upon learning his fate. "There were a lot of rumors going around about trades or them taking someone else, and I said I could be happy playing anywhere. But in the back of my mind, all along, I knew I wanted to play in Dallas. It's a good situation for me."

Jones, of course, was elated. "We think Troy is the best player in the country," he said.

And he was paid as if he were the best, receiving a six-year, $11.2 million deal that made him the highest-paid rookie in National Football League history. Before Aikman, Vinny Testaverde, Miami's Heisman Trophy–winning quarterback, was the highest-paid rookie when he was the No. 1 pick by the Tampa Bay Bucs in 1987 and signed for $8.2 million over six years.

Testaverde hadn't lived up to his billing when Aikman signed his contract—and he never did develop into a consistent performer. The memory of other first-round quarterbacks who proved to be disappointments was always in the minds of concerned Dallas fans.

Signing the contract was the easy part. In July 1989, the Cowboys picked up another quarterback when they chose University of Miami star Steve Walsh, who led Johnson's Hurricanes to a national title, in the NFL's supplemental draft. There was speculation Walsh might challenge Aikman for the starting job, but it died down when Aikman showed his stuff in preseason.

Perhaps the biggest problem facing Aikman was that he was joining a poor team whose fans were not used to losing.

He was labeled "The Franchise," worked for a new coach whom he had twice rejected, and Cowboys' fans were still enraged over Landry's firing.

But Aikman could do nothing about that. All he could do was prepare himself for the coming season, one he knew would be filled with ups and downs, mostly downs.

While UCLA had a 20-4 record with Aikman at quarterback, wins didn't come easy with the Cowboys.

Not only were they trying to rebound from one of their poorest seasons, they were going to do it with an untested quarterback in Aikman. This added even more pressure to the kid from Henryetta. It is rare indeed for a rookie to start his first professional football game.

In the first game of the season, against the New Orleans Saints, Aikman was overwhelmed in a 28–0 loss. Still, he gave indications the Cowboys had made a wise investment.

In fact, after his first two games, a sports columnist from the *Fort Worth Star Telegram* wrote: "He has played with such poise that sometimes it seems difficult to remember whether Troy Aikman has been the starting quarterback of the Dallas Cowboys for two games or 10 years."

High praise for a rookie who had four interceptions and one touchdown pass. But sometimes, the real story is not in the numbers, and that was the case with Aikman.

He was confident and composed when everything around him was breaking down, especially his pass protection. He was quick to pick up defenses, able to find the open receiver, and to take a hit and get back up. He mastered the offense, from the short, medium, and deep routes to the shotgun and the running game.

"I've had rookie quarterbacks before," quarterbacks coach Jerry Rhome said. "None compare to Troy. He's very alert during the game as to what's going on around him and what people across the line of scrimmage are trying to do. That's why in two games he's only made a couple of mistakes."

Aikman, meanwhile, tried to remain optimistic.

"I don't know what other rookies have felt like," he said. "I feel young out there, like I'm seeing a lot of things for the first time. I'm sure I'll be more comfortable and confident in the years to come than I am now."

It got worse before it got better.

In his fourth game, Aikman broke his left

Aikman was not an immediate success as a rookie. A broken finger also kept him on the sidelines for six weeks. During that streak, the Cowboys won their only game of the year.

index finger and was out for six weeks, missing five games. Walsh moved into the starter's role, with veteran Babe Laufenberg as the backup.

In his first game back, against the Phoenix Cardinals, Aikman took one of the hardest hits he'd ever taken. And it came on an 80-yard touchdown pass for the go-ahead score in what would have been his first NFL win.

Aikman, in his book *Troy Aikman: Things Change* described what happened:

"Blood dripped from my ear as I lay unconscious on the football field in 1989 . My moment of glory faded to black as a Phoenix Cardinal delivered a crushing blow. I was knocked out for eight minutes. Phoenix won on a last-minute touchdown."

Aikman came back, played the rest of the season and the Cowboys finished 1-15, again the worst record in the NFL. Aikman's on-the-job training may have looked like a mismatch, but Jimmy Johnson knew his quarterback would have the last laugh.

Aikman's final numbers? He completed 155 of 293 passes for 1,749 yards, 9 touchdowns and 18 interceptions. He was 0-11, the lowest rated quarterback in the league. He called the experience a nightmare season. "The one game we won, I was out with a broken finger," Aikman recalled. "I took so many hits, I wondered how anyone could play in the NFL more than a few years.

"I'd faced rough years before, but this season was the worst. I dreamed so long and worked so hard to be a quarterback in the NFL, but nothing went right. My dream turned into a nightmare."

Before the 1990 season started, the Cowboys

began loading up their roster, drafting Florida All-American running back Emmitt Smith, signing 16 free agents and making several key trades, including one for tight end Jay Novacek.

Expectations were high and Johnson was ready for a winning season. Things started slowly, though.

After a 20–3 loss to the Cardinals on October 14, the Cowboys were 2-4 and feeling down. Aikman hit only 9 of 25 passes, was intercepted once and sacked four times as Dallas had a club-record low 100 yards on offense. After 10 games, the Cowboys were 3-7 and both Aikman and Smith were frustrated with an offense that had gone two straight games without a touchdown. In fact, Aikman publicly criticized the offensive game plan.

In the eleventh game, Aikman asserted himself and completed 17 of 32 passes for 303 yards and 3 touchdowns in a much-needed 24–21 win over the Los Angeles Rams. "I've still got a lot of learning to do; this hasn't been a spectacular year for me," Aikman said afterward.

That victory was the start of a four-game winning streak that put the Cowboys in position to make the playoffs for the first time since 1985. On Thanksgiving, the Cowboys beat the Redskins 27-17 and Aikman said: "We're not just trying to have a break-even year. We're looking to win the rest of our games and finish 9-7."

The next week, Aikman directed two 80-yard scoring drives in the second half—at one time completing 11 passes in a row—in a 17–13 win over New Orleans, which earlier in the season acquired Walsh in a trade. The victory gave Dallas its first

A win over the New York Giants in 1991 showed that Aikman was a star quarterback and that the Cowboys were getting better.

back-to-back home wins since 1985.

The Cowboys were at 7-7 entering their crucial game against the Philadelphia Eagles, but injury hit Aikman again. Less than five minutes into the game, he separated his right shoulder when tackled by defensive end Clyde Simmons. The Eagles won 17–3 and the Cowboys' playoff chances hung on the arm of Laufenberg.

With Aikman out, the Atlanta Falcons beat Dallas 26–7 on the final weekend. The Cowboys could have backed into the playoffs with a Rams' victory over the Saints in the final regular-season game on Monday night. The game went into overtime, but the Saints won and the Cowboys' season was over.

In 1991, there was renewed hope, and nothing short of the playoffs was acceptable. Aikman was now a seasoned veteran, but coming off another injury. Norv Turner was the new offensive coordinator and the Cowboys again drafted well, making Outland Trophy winner Russell Maryland the No. 1 pick. Another key move was the acquisition of backup quarterback Steve Beuerlein from the Los Angeles Raiders.

After four games, the Cowboys were 2-2 going into a critical test against the New York Giants. Aikman came through, throwing a 23-yard scoring pass to Michael Irvin with 2:13 left in the game to give the Cowboys a 21–16 victory over the previous year's Super Bowl champions.

"There is no question this is the biggest victory," Aikman said. "It was one of the teams we needed to beat to establish ourselves. I just hope I can play here long enough where a victory over the Giants won't be considered a novelty."

By the end of November, the Cowboys were 6-5 entering another crucial contest—against the undefeated Washington Redskins at RFK Stadium.

Aikman had his Cowboys ahead 14–7 with 12:54 left in the third quarter.

Aikman, who had been sacked five times in the first half, was 13 of 19 for 204 yards and a touchdown before being sandwiched between linebacker Monte Coleman and end Charles Mann just as he released the ball (a 27-yard completion to Alvin Martin). The quarterback suffered a torn ligament in his right knee. Beuerlein came on and the Cowboys hung on to win 21–14, but Aikman was out for the season.

The Cowboys, with Beuerlein at quarterback, won their next four games—against the Pittsburgh Steelers, New Orleans Saints, Philadelphia Eagles, and Atlanta Falcons—finished 11-5, and made the playoffs for the first time since 1985.

Aikman meanwhile was cheering from the sidelines and working his knee back into shape. In fact, he thought he was ready to start in the playoffs against the Chicago Bears. When Johnson said he was sticking with Beuerlein, Aikman could have made an issue of it, but chose not to.

"There's a time and a place to say something, but it would be selfish on my part to do something that would hurt or distract the team," he said. "I felt I was ready to play last week."

The Cowboys won their first playoff game since 1983, beating the Chicago Bears 17–13 in an NFC divisional game. The next week, though, the Cowboys' season came tumbling down in a 38–6 loss to the Detroit Lions. Aikman played the second half in an effort to spark Dallas, but was unable to give them much of a lift. Although he completed 11 passes for 114 yards, missing five games showed.

He fumbled once and lost two snaps from center.

"I don't think I gave us much of a spark," Aikman said.

He was right, but he knew he had healed and would be back to lead the Cowboys the following season.

5

THE COWBOYS: THE CHAMPIONSHIP YEARS

$\mathbf{A}$ikman started the 1992 season with a clean slate, his shoulder separation a thing of the past, his unhappiness with not playing much of the postseason ancient history.

He started strong and never looked back, leading Dallas to victories in eight of its first nine games, including a season-opening 23–10 win over the Super Bowl champion Redskins and a 34–28 win over the Giants the next week.

Aikman was 40 of 66 for 454 yards and 3 touchdowns in those games and played with the resolve of someone looking to play in the Super Bowl, which was set for the Rose Bowl in Pasadena, California, the site of his most disappointing college defeats.

He also had two wonderful games against the Phoenix Cardinals. In Week 3, he threw a career-best 87-yard scoring pass to Michael Irvin—one of three touchdown passes to Irvin—that was the fourth longest in club history. Eight games later he completed a season-high

Aikman can scramble when he has to.

Jimmy Johnson pats his quarterback on the back after Aikman led the Cowboys to a win over the San Francisco 49ers in the 1993 NFC championship game.

25 passes, including two touchdowns in a 16–10 win over the Cardinals.

That game began a string of five straight in which he threw at least two touchdown passes—the longest in franchise history since Danny White had a six-game streak in 1983. "Mike just kept getting open," the humble Aikman said. "The 87-yarder, though, WAS something."

In Week 7, the Cowboys beat the Kansas City Chiefs 17–10 (Aikman was a pinpoint 21 of 29 for 192 yards and a touchdown) and took over sole possession of first place in the NFC East for the first time since 1986. The division was widely regarded as the toughest in football, as the Giants and Redskins had recently won Super Bowls and the Eagles were always a tough team to beat, too. Coach Jimmy Johnson felt prompted to proclaim: "I think we have a Super Bowl-caliber team."

Two weeks later, Aikman was dishing out praise to Emmitt Smith after a 20–10 victory over the Eagles that boosted the Cowboys 7-1 and avenged their only loss.

"I've never seen anything like him," Aikman said after Smith carried 30 times for 163 yards. "Some of the holes he picks through, you think he's buried on the bottom somewhere, and then he's squirting out the other end."

In one of the better Cowboy comebacks under Aikman, Dallas trailed the Denver Broncos 27–24 in the final minutes. Aikman, though, completed 7 of 8 passes and Smith scored on a 3-yard run to cap a 77-yard scoring drive with 2:47 left. The Cowboys won 31–27.

It was the seventh time Aikman had led the Cowboys from behind in the fourth quarter to win.

The next week, he reached the 10,000-yard plateau in his 52nd pro game, faster than any other quarterback in team history. The Cowboys (13-3) went on to win their first NFC East title since 1985, finishing with a club-record 13 wins. And Aikman was simply superb, completing 302 of 473 passes for 3,445 yards and 23 touchdowns and being named to the Pro Bowl team again.

In the playoffs, Aikman took his game to an even higher level. He completed an amazing 61 of 89 passes for 795 yards, 8 touchdowns and 0 interceptions for an amazing 126.4 quarterback rating.

In Dallas's 30–20 win over the San Francisco 49ers in the NFC championship game, Aikman was 24 of 34 for 322 yards and 2 touchdowns on a wet field at Candlestick Park.

With the score tied 10–10 at the half, Aikman took the Cowboys on second-half scoring marches of 78, 79, and 79 yards to keep his team in control.

At one point, the 49ers closed to 24–20, but Aikman fired a pass to Alvin Harper, who raced 70 yards to the 9 yardline. On a third-and-goal from the 6, Aikman threw a pass to Kelvin Martin for a touchdown to ensure the victory and a trip to the Super Bowl.

"I thought Troy did a fantastic job," Johnson raved.

All Aikman could say was: "We're very excited about reaching the Super Bowl."

Two weeks later at the Rose Bowl, before an exuberant crowd of 98,374, Aikman passed himself into history with the game of a lifetime. He started slowly, but warmed up enough to wipe out all his bad memories of the 1987 Rose Bowl and become the Most Valuable Player in the 1993 Super Bowl.

He completed 22 of 30 passes for 273 yards and 4 touchdowns—two came only 18 seconds apart—as the Cowboys defeated the Buffalo Bills 52–17 for their first NFL championship since 1978.

"This game meant everything to me," Aikman said. "It's a tremendous amount of weight off my shoulders. No matter what happens for the rest of my career, at least I can say I took my team to a Super Bowl and I was able to win."

He said he started slowly because he got caught up in the hype.

"I was just thinking, 'Stay relaxed. Don't make the game bigger than what it appears,'" he said. "Going out and seeing the pageantry of it, I had to talk myself into relaxing. Early on, I was caught up in the moment and too anxious. I didn't feel real comfortable until midway through the second quarter. Then I got into a groove."

After the game he and his teammates were in the groove, too. Aikman filmed an "I'm going to Disneyland," commercial, went to a team celebration in Santa Monica, hit the early morning talk shows and then was whisked off to Hawaii for the Pro Bowl.

Even in Hawaii, things remained hectic for Aikman. He had a commitment to be back in Dallas for his charitable Aikman Foundation. His Pro Bowl coaches, from the 49ers, told him he would come out of the game after the first series of the second half. The game ran late, Aikman left early and made his flight.

Coach George Seifert complained he didn't know where Aikman was. The quarterback, who was fined $5,000 by the league, was embarrassed and made a public apology later in the week to the 400,000 people who showed up for the Super Bowl parade in Dallas.

On March 5, Aikman and his teammates had the honor of being received by President Bill Clinton in the White House. Two days later, Aikman was back in his hometown of Henryetta, Oklahoma, for a one-convertible parade down Main Street.

It was Troy Aikman Day, and his high school basketball coach, William Skimbo, recalled: "Troy's like a rock star. People have put him on a pedestal and rightfully so. He's a good guy, a good player, and he's good for this community."

A quarterback loves having great receivers. Tight end Jay Novacek and wide receiver Michael Irvin have often made Aikman look good.

Now the 1993 season was about ready to start, and there were several changes in the Cowboys' system. Defensive coordinator Dave Wannstedt left to replace Mike Ditka as coach of the Chicago Bears. And then there was the big Emmitt Smith holdout, where the NFL's leading rusher the past two years wanted more money than owner Jerry Jones was willing to part with.

Smith missed the first two games, and the Cowboys lost both, to the Redskins and the Bills. No NFL team ever started 0-2 and went to the Super Bowl. A seven-game winning streak ensued, Aikman had an even better season than

Aikman set three NFL records with his passing in the two Super Bowls.

he did the previous year, and the Cowboys won the NFC East at 12-4 and returned for another Super Bowl matchup against the Bills.

While the previous Super Bowl season was a dream come true, this season was one crisis after another. In the 31–9 win over the Giants on November 7, Aikman suffered yet another injury, this one a left hamstring problem that forced him to miss the next two games. Before he left, though, he was 11 of 13, including touchdown passes of 28 and 50 yards to Alvin Harper, and Dallas led 17–6.

When he returned to the lineup, the Cowboys were 7-3 entering their Thanksgiving game against the Dolphins. Dallas had the game won 14–13, but after the Cowboys blocked a field goal attempt in the final seconds, Leon Lett mistakenly went after the ball and Miami recovered, allowing Pete Stoyanovich another chance. This time, his kick was good and the Cowboys fell to 7-4.

But with Aikman and Smith excelling, the Cowboys won their final four games and were on a roll heading to the playoffs. The most compelling game was the regular-season finale against the Giants. The teams were tied for the division lead and the Cowboys won in overtime 16–13 as Smith had one of the most courageous performances in memory, running for 168 yards and catching 10 passes for 61 more despite separating his right shoulder with 1:58 left in the half.

Smith won his third rushing title and Aikman had another brilliant season, completing 271 of 392 passes for 3,100 yards and 15 touchdowns. Again, Aikman was named to the Pro Bowl, this time as a starter.

The playoffs saw Aikman on his game. In the 27–17 victory over the Green Bay Packers, Aikman was 28 of 37 for 302 yards and 3 touchdowns. He was 14 of 18 for 177 yards and 2 touchdowns against the Steve Young–led 49ers in the NFC title game before suffering a concussion early in the third quarter. The Cowboys won 38–21, but Aikman was hurting.

In his book, Aikman discussed what happened: "Strangely, I don't remember anything about the game. That's because the knee of 300-pound 49er Dennis Brown smacked into the side of my helmet.... I remained awake in a haze of confusion on the sidelines and had trouble remembering things."

After a night at Baylor University Medical center, someone asked him if he knew the site of the Super Bowl.

"Henryetta?"

By Tuesday, he had to be ready to travel to Atlanta to get ready for another run at a Super Bowl title. Unlike most years, when teams had two weeks to prepare, there was only one week to get ready.

Aikman was not himself at practice, nor in the first half against the Bills, who led 13–6. But the Cowboys took control in the second half, Aikman snapped out of his funk and completed 19 of 27 passes for 207 yards, and Dallas won 30–13 for its second Super Bowl win in a row.

Aikman's two-year postseason performance set three NFL records—highest rating (111.2), completion percentage (71.1%), and yards per attempt (8.53).

BACK WITH BARRY

After a second straight Super Bowl victory, the Cowboys' off season was one of the most contentious in club history, even more testy than the firing of Tom Landry.

In the months before training camp, a feud between owner Jerry Jones and coach Jimmy Johnson boiled over during drinks one night in Florida. The result? Johnson resigned and Jones hired former Oklahoma University coach Barry Switzer, who had been out of coaching since 1989.

Aikman, of course, knew all about Switzer. Troy had decided to join Oklahoma and play for Switzer instead of joining Jimmy Johnson at Oklahoma State University. Johnson had soon moved to the University of Florida—where he won a national championship. Johnson had been interested in having Aikman play for him at Florida when Troy soured on the Sooners after Switzer made it clear he was starting

In the 1994 NFC championship game, Aikman was knocked to the ground more than a dozen times.

Artie Smith (number 95) checks out Aikman after the downed quarterback received a knee to the head in the 1994 NFC game against the 49ers.

another quarterback.

Also, offensive coordinator Norv Turner had left Dallas to become coach of the Washington Redskins, with the low-key and highly respected Ernie Zampese replacing him. That made it three offensive coordinators in four years for Aikman. In addition, Aikman had another new backup in Rodney Peete, who replaced Bernie Kosar, who replaced Steve Beuerlein.

Aikman, though, had by this time developed into a team leader and was prepared to do whatever was needed to win it all again.

"You look around here, and there's no doubt we have the talent," he said. "What it comes down to is we believe in ourselves and we believe in this football team. I know it's not going to come down to what I can do. It's going to come down to what we all do. Yes, there's a lot of pressure. But that pressure is on all of us, not just the quarterback. That's the kind of pressure that makes everyone perform better."

With Emmitt Smith, Michael Irvin, Alvin Harper, and Jay Novacek back, along with several key defensive stars, Switzer was expected to not only get the Cowboys back to the Super Bowl, but to lead the team to an unprecedented third straight Super Bowl triumph.

It very nearly happened.

Once again, the Cowboys started out with a bang, beating the Pittsburgh Steelers 26–9, with Aikman hitting 21 of 32 passes for 245 yards and a touchdown. It was exactly what the team needed to open the Switzer regime.

"If we started off wrong it would raise a lot of doubts and concerns and that wouldn't have been good for the team," Aikman said. "It wasn't bad for an opener, but there is still a lot of room to get better."

After a three-point win over the Houston Oilers, the Cowboys lost in overtime to the Detroit Lions, 20–17, and Irvin was critical of the offense, claiming he wasn't being used enough. Aikman wasn't happy.

"I don't tolerate that," he said. "Michael should be wise enough to realize he will get the ball."

The offense got on track October 9 against the Cardinals as Aikman threw two first-half touchdown passes en route to a 38–3 win.

Aikman said it was the Cowboys' best game since the Super Bowl.

"We played as good today as we've played in a long time," said Aikman, who hit on 16 of 22 passes for 231 yards. "Our receivers did a great job against Buddy's defense."

Even Smith got to rest, leaving at halftime in favor of Lincoln Coleman. Aikman left after three quarters as the Cowboys improved to 4-1.

The following Sunday against the Eagles, Aikman showed why he ranks among the league's best quarterbacks. After completing only two of his first nine passes, Aikman got positive yardage on 10 of his next 14 attempts. Despite being sacked twice and knocked down a dozen times, he threw touchdown passes of 16 yards to Harper and 14 yards to Novacek in a 24–13 win that gave Dallas sole possession of first place in the NFC East.

"If Troy goes nuts on you when things go bad then it's all over," Switzer said. "That's why I call him Stone Face. He never changes expression and he never has any panic. He just hangs in there and gets the job done."

The next week, Aikman suffered a concussion in the first quarter against the Cardinals when linebacker Wilber Marshall slammed his helmet into Aikman's face, gashing his chin and tongue so severely stitches were required. Aikman gave Dallas a 7–0 lead with a 15-yard scoring pass to Harper. Aikman left after the touchdown pass and Peete finished off a 28–21 win.

The Cowboys improved to 7-1 with a close-call 23–20 win over the winless Cincinnati Bengals. In a moment that raised fears in football fans across the nation, Aikman took another blow to the head from linebacker James Francis. Francis was flagged for a "roughing the passer" penalty.

"He got a good lick on me," Aikman said,"but I came out OK." Indeed, Aikman threw two touchdowns to rally the Cowboys.

Against the powerhouse 49ers two weeks later, Aikman, who was 23 of 42 for 339 yards, was picked off three times and it was determined he played with an injured right thumb, hurt during practice but unreported. The 49ers won 21–14 and gained the advantage for the homefield throughout the playoffs.

"It was not a factor in the turnovers," Aikman said of his sore thumb. "It would be wrong to suggest it had a major effect on my performance."

The next week was another problem for Aikman. He suffered a strained left knee in the first half against the Redskins that would force him to miss the next two games.

Against the Packers on Thanksgiving, third-string quarterback Jason Garrett, a rookie from Princeton University, led the team to a 42–31 win. The next week, Peete, who injured his thumb replacing Aikman two weeks earlier, led Dallas over the Eagles.

The Cowboys' season had been so good that they coasted a little at the end. Aikman came back for the final three games, which included two losses, one to the Giants in the season finale when Aikman played just five series. Nevertheless, their 12-4 record gained the NFC East title.

Aikman pointed out that the Cowboys came close to winning 15 of their 16 games.

"The first three losses might have been wins

Troy Aikman is still young. Who knows how many more Super Bowl trophies he'll wind up with?

if three plays had gone our way—a referee's call, one pass, and an extra inch," he said. Aikman completed 233 of 366 passes for 2,676 yards and 13 touchdowns for the season.

Before the playoffs, Aikman made his peace with Switzer, saying "He's a player's coach. He's relaxed the players and the coaches. And he will express himself if he has to. I think he's done a good job, so far."

In their first playoff game, the Cowboys eliminated the Packers 30–23, with Aikman completing 23 of 30 passes for 337 yards and 2 touchdowns. Next up—the San Francisco 49ers at Candlestick Park. Before the start of the season, San Francisco had stocked up on talent. Joining such stars as Steve Young and Jerry Rice were defensive Pro Bowlers Richard Dent, Deion Sanders, and Ken Norton, Jr., late of the Cowboys. The 49ers were considered the favorites to win the game—especially as they had home-field advantage, but most people expected a close game.

San Francisco jumped out to a 21–0 lead after only 7½ minutes. The 49ers couldn't do anything wrong and the Cowboys couldn't do anything right. But Dallas refused to give up.

Aikman showed his offense could score on any-one, and put together four impressive scoring drives. Throwing the ball far more often than usual, Aikman ended the game 30 of 53 for 380 yards and 2 touchdowns. Still, the Cowboys wound up losing 38–28 to end their season one win short of going to the Super Bowl for a record third consecutive time. It was Aikman's first postseason defeat after seven victories.

After the game, Aikman found 49ers quarter-back Steve Young. "I'm happy for you," he told him. "Good luck against San Diego." (Young didn't need luck; his 49ers beat the Chargers by a lopsided score.)

Aikman said he was disappointed with the loss, but was still proud of the way his team responded throughout a tumultuous season.

"Some say our 1994 season was not a suc-cess," he said. "I never will. I'm more proud of the '94 team than our Super Bowl teams. We were champions over change."

There's one doubt about Troy Aikman's future. Clearly, he remains a top-caliber quar-terback leading a team loaded with excellent players. But in the few years he's been a pro player, he's taken many hard shots. Blows to the head can have a cumulative effect, and Aikman has suffered several known concus-sions—and possibly more minor concussions that were never diagnosed. Aikman himself has suggested he might not play much longer if he continues to suffer such abuse.

This has had the leading minds at the National Football League staying up nights. If a big, strong, mobile quarterback such as Aikman effectively risks his health every time he steps onto the field, what dangers are the smaller, slower quarterbacks facing? In the past, the league has changed the rules trying to protect quarterbacks. Referees have been instructed to enforce these rules strictly so that some of the most popular players aren't forced to retire before their time. But nothing can change the basic fact that in football, 260-pound linebackers and 300-pound defensive ends are paid millions of dollars to knock quarterbacks to the ground. No helmet could ever be designed to protect a quarterback from these very types of assault.

Aikman lives on a ranch outside Dallas. "Sometimes people paint me to be a true-to-life cowboy," said the country boy from Henryetta, Oklahoma. "I can't even ride a horse."

Whether Aikman has another 10 years in the pros, or whether he devotes the rest of his life to the ranch, he has already achieved more than most quarterbacks can even dream of. He's starred in the Pro Bowl, won two Super Bowls and showed that, like the great Joe Montana, he's at his best in the big games.

CHRONOLOGY

1966   Troy Kenneth Aikman born, November 21.

1984   Agrees to attend the University of Oklahoma and play for Coach Barry Switzer.

1988   After transferring to UCLA, Aikman leads team to victory in the Aloha Bowl.

1989   For the second straight year, the Bruins miss the Rose Bowl; Aikman leads them to victory in Cotton Bowl. Dallas Cowboys choose Aikman as the number one player in the college draft.

1992   Reaches the 10,000-yard plateau faster than any Cowboy quarterback; is named to the Pro Bowl.

1993   Leads team to victory over the Buffalo Bills in the Super Bowl; is named MVP of the Super Bowl.

1994   Despite several injuries, again leads Cowboys to victory over the Buffalo Bills in the Super Bowl.

STATISTICS

TROY AIKMAN
Dallas Cowboys

YEAR	ATT	CMP	YDS	PCT	INT	TD
1989	293	155	1749	52.9	18	9
1990	399	226	2579	56.6	18	11
1991	363	237	2754	65.3	10	11
1992	473	302	3445	63.8	14	23
1993	392	271	3100	69.1	6	15
1994	361	233	2676	64.5	12	13
TOTALS	2281	1424	16303	62.4	78	82
PLAYOFFS						
1991	16	11	114	68.8	1	0
1992	89	61	795	68.5	0	8
1993	82	61	686	74.4	3	5
1994	83	53	717	62.4	4	4
TOTALS	270	186	1592	68.9	8	17

ATT   attempts
CMP   completions
YDS   yards
PCT   percentages
INT   interceptions
TD   touchdowns

SUGGESTIONS FOR FURTHER READING

Aikman, Troy, with Greg Brown. Troy Aikman: *Things Change*. Dallas: Taylor Publishing Co. 1995.

Bayless, Skip. *The Boys*. New York: Pocket Books, 1993.

Fisher, Mike. *The Boys are Back: The Return of the Dallas Cowboys*. New York: Summit Books, 1993.

Shapiro, Leonard. *The Dallas Cowboys*. New York: St. Martin's Press, 1993.

ABOUT THE AUTHOR

Richard Rosenblatt is a national editor in sports for The Associated Press in New York. He has covered the National Football League for 15 years. He has two children, David and Erica, and lives in Floral Park, New York.

INDEX

PICTURE CREDITS
AP/Wide World Photos: 2, 8, 11, 14, 26, 29, 32, 44, 46, 49, 50, 52, 54, 58; Herman L. Brown, Okmulgee, OK: 16, 19, 22, 37, 40; UPI/Bettmann: 34.